I0542783

WHEN CAN WE BE SOFT

POEMS OF FEMALE RESILIENCE

BOBBIE ISABEL

Copyright © 2023 B. Isabel Writes LLC
All rights reserved.
ISBN: 9781961045019

❀ Created with Vellum

DEDICATION

This collection is for all of us who are stronger and more resilient than we ever thought we'd be and are tired. May we find a soft place to land where we are safe enough to be vulnerable and heal from the blows this hard world has dealt us.

INTRODUCTION AND CONTENT
WARNING

When I began pulling this collection together, I knew I wanted to capture the struggles I have experienced being born female and growing up as a woman. I am constantly reminded of the adage, "What doesn't kill us makes us stronger," and I always wondered why strength was considered a positive consolation prize. The world is a hard place. Do we not deserve the opportunity, the space, to be soft?

When we have no choice but to survive, resilience is not a peaceful outcome but rather one built on hyper-vigilance. The more ways in which we've fought to survive, the more cracks in our foundation. In my case, the more I thought I was healing because I could find moments of hope, the more cracks I found in the mask I had worn all these years. When it finally shattered, I was once again returned to survival mode trying to find out who I was behind the mask. The strength everyone saw and attributed was a facade.

Does this mean that we cannot survive this hard world through resilient hope? Absolutely not! It does mean, though, that we need and deserve the opportunity to be soft, to have days of ease where we can let our guard down and just be. We know through experience that history repeats itself, and if we are too tired to fight the same battles again, we'll never find those moments of reprieve.

In these pages, I examine various topics related to this hard world, our means of survival, the resilience we develop, and the hope we still seem to find. These topics include external and internal messages, societal and familial expectations, and relationships. Every poem, even those focused on hope for the future, come from a heavy place shrouded in pain and anger. Some of these poems and topics may be difficult to read. You know yourself and your current state. Stop reading if you need to and come back when you can.

PART I
POEMS OF A HARD WORLD

THREE GHOSTS OF MISOGYNY

The ghosts of misogyny rear
their heads
in calls for a return to the
good ol' days

The days of yore
when marital rape
was not only expected
but a spectator sport
ghosts of cheerful laughter
accompanying the bride
carried to her bed
stripped of her dignity
covered in a white sheet
soon red from his rutting
proof of her lost innocence
and the promise of
expected compliance
until death shall she depart

The cry might be for
those nostalgic times
where a woman was likely
to die on the birth bed
of any one of her
multitudinous children
or to mourn their loss
before they'd learned to walk

Maybe it's a call for
more modern times
when my grandmother
needed a co-signer
to buy her own house
the year before I was born
because women still could not
own property or have credit
Maybe they want to return
to a time when our grandmothers
stayed in loveless
and often abusive marriages
because they could not legally be
independently secure

Yes, the ghosts of misogyny rear
their heads
in calls for a return to
the good ol' days
in the hopes society
will give them free reign
to terrorize us anew
while we're too tired
to fight this battle again

SILENCE IN WHITE

freshly fallen snow
silencing my screams in white
dystopian dreams

THE NIGHTMARE

Time stands still,
as dragon fire surrounds me.
I shudder in fear at its return.
I cannot run. Hiding is useless.
I have no power here and am
too small. It stalks.
The smell of its breath,
cinder and nicotine, with a hint of
sickeningly sweet something.
I look for shelter, arms to provide safety.
No one else is there. They're never there
or never see. I close my eyes,
as it bids me touch its hardness
juxtaposed with the soft, quivering underbelly.
I do not understand its purring and cooing,
the sweet professions of love when
its caresses feel nothing like love.
I hear a scream, but it is not my own.
I try to pull away, but confusion holds me still.
His steady grunts
come in waves
from a distance.
They mix with the screams
that fill me with terror, as I'm jolted awake.
The cacophony of sounds continue. I hide in
my closet.

THE TRUTH ABOUT MONSTERS

stealing our youth and
holding life in nightmare's grip—
monsters are human

TREASURE

Treasure, dear child,
is not found in coffers
marked neatly with an X,
the dream of pirates
and the powerful alike.

Treasure, young lover
is not a gift of silver rings,
promised plenitude, or
explosive fireworks
of impassioned embraces.

Treasure, instead,
is hope in a world
full of misadventures
and disparities where pirates
are vilified and the powerful
venerated for the same actions.

Treasure is hope
that love will endure
far beyond lustful demands,
embers glowing like
fireflies in the evening fields of
comfortable appreciation.

Hope is a treasure
easily squandered
in streets of despair
after the money is spent
and the flames flicker out
when we have nothing else
left.

MOTHER'S TRAINING

Stand straight.
Chin up.
Never let them see you sweat.
A lady has poise,
pandering to the masses,
remaining aloof, yet
presenting a smile.
Stuck in the perfect pleats
between
taking myself too seriously
and
exposing the hot mess inside.

A CAUTIONARY TALE

Follow the path.
Stay in your lane.
Do not detour.
Ignore the scenic route.
Maintain your speed.
Veer neither left nor right.
Keep your eye on the prize.
End in sight.
Future decided.
Fastest way is through.
Only one way out.
No U-turns allowed.
Make us proud.

CATHEDRAL AESTHETIC

Columns and pillars
Both separation and reinforcement
Holding up pedestals of morality
Hiding imperfections in ritual

Spired beacon to the lost
Exchanging hope for tithes
Inequities for prayer
Promises of salvation for trauma

Pulpits, pews, and pedophiles
Grace, guilt, and greasy palms
Benediction, benevolence, and bigotry
Faith, friendships, and famine

Perception of a dual image
Two-faced cloture gates
Giving and taking away
Waxing and waning on whimsy

Aesthetic priorities in architecture
Show outward pride
Inner darkness bathed in shadows
Projected outward

SELF-ESTEEM BY THE NUMBERS

6, 8, 12, 14...A math story
we all could share.
Jeans are all the rage.
Everyone wants a pair.
Stone-washed, acid-washed,
weathered at the knees...
get the latest style
or else everyone will tease.

Store A has the brand
all your friends have loved.
Try them on, 6s fit
your body like a glove.
They just don't have the style
nor the color that you want,
so you head to Boutique B
for the jeans you want to flaunt.

Boutique B has got the goods
The color and the brand,
but 6s must be popular
for they have no pairs on hand.
Here, try this off-name denim,
though they run a little small.
Not 6s, 8s, nor 12s can fit.
Let's run off to the mall.

Store to store, you make your search,
legs blue from all the dye,
until you don the perfect pair
of 14s. Then, you cry.
The size is wrong; it just can't be.
You wore 6s yesterday.
To fit right in with sense of self,
fashion makes you pay.

THE PREGNANCY DILEMMA

Don't have sex; you could get pregnant.
Don't take the pill; you'll look promiscuous.
Don't expect the dude to wear a condom.
Don't you dare consider an abortion!
Don't you think they'd make cute babies together?
Don't you think you're too young for a baby?
You're too young for sterilization; what if your future
husband wants kids?
What if you change your mind and want kids later?
You're not getting any younger; don't you want kids?
We're not getting any younger; don't we deserve grandkids?
Aren't you a little too old to be having kids?
When are you going to have another one?
What were you thinking having so many?

UNJUST

the price of aging
in unjust creases
telling your secrets
before questions are asked
life well-lived or
unbelievable hardship
written across the face of time
for all to judge as if
wrinkles were signs of
neglect and not wisdom

ENDLESS STRIVING

never good enough
seeking praise that would not come
striving for her best

INVERTED MORALITY

how much is too much—
bodies more regulated
than weapons of death

POWER AND CONTROL

Sexually active
Sexually assaulted
Sexually adept

Power over one's body
extends to the pleasures of others
who have no consequences
and don't deal with the aftermath

Too young
Too single
Too unfettered

How do you take control against the stream
of doctors discussing what ifs
as if they will ever have to decide
when you already know what you want

Swollen belly
Swollen feet
Swollen ego
The toll on a pregnant body
on both the heart and mind
matter not in the eyes
of those not living in that skin

Morally inept
Morally corrupt
Morally torn

Decisions made in an office
are easily justified against
decisions made in a kitchen
when there are already empty bellies

Don't fight
Don't cry
Don't die

The righteous travel with pitchforks
crusading for lives they'll later disdain
while the vilified argue for survival
armed only with coat hangers

MEDUSA'S LEGACY

Children are to be seen and not heard
Women no different
Guilted into a life of temperance
Of abstinence from all
Lest we be ostracized
By the gods of men
An anathema,
Snakes hissing around our heads

Medusa, too, was a victim
Of the gods' whims
Locked into a life of celibacy
Disfigurement the price of sex
Cursed to hide her form
Hunted and feared
Lust for her blood
Balanced against
Lust for her body
Rage coursing through her veins
Manifested in the glow of her eyes
The hiss of her breath
The rattle of her tail

That same rage runs through women today
Though the gods are silent
Man playing God guised in morality
Denying rights to all who might disagree
Cloaking their lust in black robes Pointing
fingers
Placing blame
Protecting their interests
Without taking responsibility
Forcing our disfigurement
For fear we might
Turn them to stone

INDIRECT CONVERSATIONS

I've always been direct
Maybe too damn blunt
But never to be rude
Or intending to affront

I like when there's no question
Of whatever do I mean
I try to say things plain as day
With communication clean

You like to beat around the bush
Ambiguity your friend
Your words have double meaning
Protecting feelings, you pretend

I cannot understand you
And question all your thoughts
Deciphering your meaning
Is much like casting lots

I think you seek protection
From accountability
For when words have no true
meaning You can say "it wasn't
me"

So, whenever I fall silent
At whatever you professed
Know I searched for hidden meaning
And my mind filled in the rest

DRIFTWOOD

Tossing in the wake
Strewn along the shore
Remnant wreckage
Of a love no more

The once mighty ship
Strength and tranquility
Danced along the landscape
A herald's fantasy

The crew maintained her visage
Hiding cracks, withered neglect
Pretending all was well
As regard turned to regret

The fateful day the tempest
Came to test their fortitude
The fragile hull splintered
As the ship came unglued

Storm-tossed across the sea
Found prone upon the sand A
warning sign to all
Of a relationship's last stand

HOUSE IN RUIN

We thought our house was sturdy
Until we cracked the foundation
With our insecurity
Until we tore off the roof
With our pride
Until we flooded the living space
With our grief
Until we burned down the walls
With our anger
Until we tended the garden
With our neglect
Until we hid the ruins
With our embarrassment

TOMORROW'S NIGHTMARE

the moment you think
today's nightmare is over
It's today again

PART II
POEMS OF SURVIVAL

BONE CORSETS

we wear the burdens
of our pasts like armor plate—
when can we be soft

NOSTALGIA

Preserved rose petals
Paper printed with red ink
Memories like thorns

Walk through the playground—
Images of childhood missed
A peace never known

EMPOWERMENT

How many of us were in the house?
Teenagers with bottles of vodka and no one home.
"Oh shit," I laughed as I slid down the cabinet to the floor,
Ripping my pants on the door handle.
We all laughed, and I just sat there.

"Who wants to play Nintendo?"
Like a siren's song, the bedrooms upstairs were calling us.
Six of us piled in the smallest room,
The only one with a tv.
"I bet you can't beat me at Mario 3."

Alcohol pouring,
Players cussing,
Mario jumping,
Two teens creeping,
Four of us alone.

"Whoever beats me at the next level can fuck me."
Damn, I was good.
The looks of surprise.
The uncertainty of my promise.
The furious button pushing, until you won.

"Are you sure?" Yes.
"Should we ask them to leave?" They can watch.
"Should I wear a condom?" Sure.
Whether the alcohol or the act,
It was all such a blur.

I don't remember much.
I remember you fumbling for your belt.
I remember teenage boy giggles.
I remember Legos bouncing off my chest.
I don't remember your name.

Had you known how many grown men
Wanted what I was giving you?
Could you imagine the years of fear that they'd take it
Before I was ready?
Did you have any idea what I was gaining?

HIGH-RISK BEHAVIOR

How do you know
How far to go?

Walking the track
Train at your back

You're not alone
When you're not home

Childhood abuse
Gave an excuse

Searching for calm
Adrenalin balm

Sneaking out late
Testing your fate

Lost teenager
Aged predator

Run out of town
Florida bound

Opening legs
Too many kegs

Sex on display Small
price to pay

Running from pain
With liquid grain

Can't remember
Being sober

Stealing the cash
Growing the stash

Slap on the wrist
Taking a fist

Running t'ward death
Just out of breath

Driving home drunk
Thoughts in the trunk

Can't give a fuck
Testing your luck

Aren't you scared yet
Of a lost bet?

NOBODY COULD HAVE KNOWN

Nobody could have known
The pain behind her smiling eyes
The shiver of fear
Each time a door opened
Unexpected
Literal and proverbial
The way she longed to articulate
The trauma
The discomfort
The confusion
To empathetic ears
If not for the grip of terror
On her throat
Reminder that her last attempt
Turned friend
Predator
Doubling the danger
Minimizing the safe directions to turn
Until she was frozen
Smile in place

AIR OF SOPHISTICATION

Champagne glasses clinking
Cheap wine mimosas
Knock-off Gucci bags
Carrying maxed out credit cards
Bargain basement pretense
Clothed in second-hand design
Hiding in plain sight
At out-of-league events
Banishing self-deprecation
With an air of sophistication
Hoping the guise holds
Hometown forgotten
Name changed
Allure added
Pygmalion
Escape
Alone
Lost

PROTECTIVENESS

I heard your voice before I saw your face.
It had been years, and yet I felt your presence.
I froze. I heard a laugh, a greeting. It wasn't mine.
I looked down at my child, smiling at me,
looking for her grandmother who sounded so happy.
I could almost smell you; you were so close.
Your sickeningly sweet smell still haunts me.
Your voice brought back memories I thought long buried.
I couldn't turn.
I wanted to be sick.
I wanted to scream.
I wanted to run.
I stood still, like a deer in the forest when a branch cracks.
When she called my name, asking if I remembered you, I
nearly bolted. Instead, I lifted my chin and started to turn.
The etiquette conditioning so strong that I almost smiled.
Until she said, "And this is my granddaughter..."
I never knew protection; I was never protected.
In that moment, I knew protectiveness, and
I walked away.

SELF-CARE

protecting others
becoming second nature
don't forget yourself

LOST IN THE IVY

Many of us are driven by fear
Hoping to stand out, yet
Longing to fade into the background
Secluded from prying eyes
While putting our lives on display
We stand in the sun
Statues unyielding
Suspended, bronze tarnished
Years etched by vines
Taking root around us
Climbing our immovable facades
Appearing as accessories of time
Histories adorning us in starlight
Growing with the wind, and sun,
And rain washing us away
Until we are no longer more than
A frame for others' memories

GRIEF

glimpses of time lost
staggering between teardrops
memories unfold

screaming silent sobs
forgetting to breathe until
the pain fades again

YOUR SILENCE WHISPERS

Your Silence Whispers
Into the recesses of my psyche
Screaming obscenities
Into the void of insecurities

PREGNANT PAUSES

Anticipation is a calm lake
or a bubbling sulfuric spring,
reaction held by surface tension,
steam showing what is to come.

You wait both excited and anxious,
frantically searching the facade
expecting the piercing screech,
yet all remains silent.

A single external movement
of word or deed,
an imperceivable internal image,
can trigger an explosion

The spouts of rage touching
everything within reach,
the quaking subsides returning
tension to just under the surface

CONFRONTATION

Wide open or completely shut down
There is no comfortable medium
There is no moment of equilibrium
There is no self-advocation
Only self-preservation
Only self-manipulation
Only splintered communication
In the face of confrontation

Mother's lessons in etiquette
Remaining silent a safer bet
Remaining poised a better look
Save yourself from the right hook
From words of wisdom
Disguised as fists
Reckoning that love exists
When the mark
You clearly missed

Take the blame
Apologize
Deep breaths in
Close your eyes
Ignore the signs
Flags waved red

Hold it all
Inside your head
Until your rage comes boiled up
Volcano spew your thoughts erupt
Hurtling screams left to right
Proving that you lost the fight

Doubting yourself
Guilt creeps in
In your heart and through your mind
Mindful that you'll never find
A confrontation you might win
Preferring to stay silent again

WHAT DID YOU EXPECT

What did you expect?

You laughed at my fears
And expected me to stay
You ridiculed my dreams
And expected me to stay
You shunned my affection
And expected me to stay
You jeered at my emotions
And expected me to stay
You lashed out in anger
And expected me to stay
You begged for forgiveness
And expected me to stay
You told me you loved me
And expected me to stay

I did the unexpected
And I left

BROKEN IN HEALING

broken in healing—
uncertainty in the wake
of struggling for air

EXHAUSTED LAMENTATIONS

Tired isn't strong enough
Exhausted gets much closer
Bone-weary describes how rough
The aches and pains take over

None of them fit the bill, though
For what happens in my mind
When my overworked brain shuts down
No more thoughts can I find

Pure emotion
Without filter
Every notion
Seems off kilter

Opened mouth
Foot inserted
Thoughts gone south
All effort disconcerted

Take a pill to dull the pain
Hoping for a slight reprieve
The only thing to keep you sane
Yet the grogginess just won't leave

So, I battle through each twinge
Push on ahead and sigh
As discomfort settles in
I watch the world dance by

RUNNING ON EMPTY

I sleep but no rest comes.
I wake exhausted but make it through the day.
Saying something's got to give sounds nice,
But you can't get blood from the stone
You used to kill two birds
While robbing Peter to pay Paul.

How long can you run on empty?

UNCERTAINTY

Uncertainty is...
self-deprecating jokes told
hidden behind laughs

INDECISION

Fog creeps in,
blanketing my mind in shadows
Along the rocks,
waves crash in consternation
with my thoughts
Cold justification and denial
lapping at my toes
while I stand
on the precipice of indecision

Thus is the space
between dreams and actions
where fear grips
beyond certain motives
Somewhere between
passion and security
lies the heart of comfort

I come to the sea
for clarity and peace
and yet
sometimes
she responds with turbulence,
a cautious reminder that
we grow through discomfort

The swell of her bosom
overflowing the shore
as my anxiety
overwhelms my ambition and
I make excuses
for staying in place
uncomfortable
and
unfulfilled

When Can We Be Soft?

PART III
POEMS OF RESILIENCE

GROWING PAINS

growing pains come
from vulnerability—
sliced layers of fear

PAPER BUTTERFLIES

Images of hopeless dreams
Hopeful wishes floating
Manifested in four words
Fairytale ending unreached.

Will you marry me?
She held her breath
Not believing the truth
Ignoring al the waving flags

Someone choosing her
Eternally tied, entwined
Like vines of thorns
Ripping at her peace.

Something just seems wrong
Not the unrequited side
But the force of feigned affection
Falsifying all likelihoods

She kept the secret
Questioning her answer
From the start
Knowing the end would come

Stuck in the guise of her own making
Afraid of the whispers
Haunted by the cost
The dress like a specter

Everything ready except the official
Frozen words build walls all around
His truth breaking through Releasing
her, transformed

Unafraid of the looks
His harsh words of self-hatred
The relieved sigh of retraction Paper
butterflies flew unfettered

BATTERED BUT UNBROKEN

Long forgotten storms
Wailed at your limbs
Driving you to the ground
Battered but unbroken
You reach toward the sky
Gnarled and twisted
Your ancient branches withered
Yet life springs forth
Seeds of evergreen
Sprout from your fingers
Demonstrating strength unmatched
Refusal to stay beaten
Seeking protection from the wind
In the arms of fate
Knowing you're not alone
The earth littered with majesty
Stolen in youth and ignored
Until someone sees your beauty

KINTSUGI

trauma-driven crack
filled with golden filigree
broken in her strength

PERSONIFICATION

She stood waiting
Against a backdrop of time
Crumbling with the weight of her tears.
Where have her knights gone?
She looked around at her ruins
The frailty of her once proud visage.
Where have the years gone?
The memory of those long forgotten
Still lay at her feet in perpetual worship.
How long before she's gone too?

MOTHER OCEAN

Drowning in seas of emotion,
I come to you.
Your waves wash over me,
gently lapping at the sand
between my toes.
Your energy soothes me.
Wading into the depths,
your vastness caresses me.
The roar of your voice
brings peace to my soul.
Even when faced with your rage,
wind howling,
water churning,
sand eroding,
your strength reinforces me.
In your presence,
I am renewed.

UNDER THE SURFACE

Waves of emotion rush forth
knocking me off my feet.
I tell myself I'm stronger than this,
built of finer stock,
capable of withstanding the onslaught,
of maintaining balance
in the shifting sands.

Sometimes, though, the tide wins
pulling me under,
tossing me around,
reminding me of its vastness
and my own vulnerability.
I rise sputtering,
lungs tight, and eyes burning.

The numbness stings the worst,
the cold rush of unexpected
nothing that envelopes the senses
daring me to hold my ground
and acclimate or be washed away,
slowly eroded as the surf recedes
and I am left a hollow shell.

Other times, though,
I dive headfirst into the churning,
screaming in defiance at the turbulence
surrounding me with anxious energy,
whispering in my ear its promise
of future destruction on the whim
of the moon's delight.

I look forward to the calm,
wading through the lace lapping my toes.
Buoyed by the unhurried movements, I
float on the rise and fall
Like sleeping breaths,
blissfully unaware of what lay
just below the surface.
Careening toward the jagged rocks,
I float in joyful peace

For the moment.

THE DENOUEMENT

In a flash, the fairytale ends
Dragons overcome dreams
The knight tarnishes
And the nightmare continues

Loneliness lengthened
Lessons learned
Loves lost

Fear of failure and forever
Locked in constant combat
Overpowering logic
Underwhelming expectations

Masks removed
Memories retained
Motivation reinforced

Hidden agendas absorb
Free spirit fettering imagination
In forgeries of books
Painted on long-forgotten scrolls

Silence screamed
Satisfaction sacrificed
Safety slashed

I TORE THE SKY APART

I tore the sky apart
Tossing clouds here
Moon and stars there
Rending wishes
With nails painted grief
Rearranging the pieces
Into a kaleidoscope
Of broken dreams
Shifting as they spin
Light and color prisms
Until the world sees
Through my tears

TEMPEST

Though the sky be gray
the thunder clash
the rivers swell
and
the wind howl
the storm seems tame
against
the tempest in her eyes.

THE RAIN NEVER STOPPED

The rain never stopped
though the clouds dissipated
and the sun shone

The rain never stopped
though the flood receded
and the roads cleared

The rain never stopped
though the river ran dry
and mud caked

The rain may have stopped
though my eyes rimmed red
and my cheeks stayed wet

THE FACADE

snake-like tendrils stretch out,
grasping for purchase
like hair in the wind
yet strong, powerful
intentional in their reach
feet firmly planted
basking in the sun
indifferent to the eyes
watching in wonder
unaware of the tension
holding her in place
a prisoner of her own strength
held there by tendrils of memory
longing to let go, yet
afraid of the horror left
in the wake of her collapse
she stands tall, proud,
hiding the cracks in her foundation

HEALING HURTS

the face you put on
changes with time regardless—
acid tears melt masks

SLEEPY YET AWAKE

The line between
Sleep and wakefulness
Is blurred as that between
Dream and nightmare
Truth and lie
Love and hate
The dichotomy is
One of two halves
Not one of polar opposites
Found on a spectrum of degree
Held by a thread of anxiety

Oh to sleep the sleep of toddlers
Where nightmares are few
Tied to entertainment
Explained away
Where truth is built
through imagination
And love is the only
Purely understood emotion
When wakefulness is
Unbound energy released
Everything new and exciting

I, however, am no toddler
My childhood dreams
Marred by trauma
Riddled with nightmares inexplicable
As I learned to search for truth
In the eyes of those who promised Me
love but took mine in vain
Now, though the nightmares
Are fewer than the heartbreaks The
lines remain blurred
As I fail to dream and yet
Cry in my sleep
Though I sleep, I never rest
My mind hyper-vigilant
Searching for the next half-truth Of
experience in tomorrow
Afraid to dream for fear
The nightmares will return
Thus, I start each morning
Sleepy but awake

I TRY...

I try to remember my safe haven
As a child walking through your doors
My saving grace
Loved
Appreciated
Untouchable
No nightmares calling with the turn of a key

I tried to forget the nightmares.

I try to forget the differences
Caring teachers inside and bullies outside
Being smart wasn't valued on the asphalt
And yet the praise carried home
Lasted longer than the admonishment to
"Fight your own battles"

I tried to forget the battles

I try to remember when the nightmares ended
Safety no longer needed
The bully raged in my own head
You still stood strong
Waiting for my return
As I pushed further away from your lockered halls

I tried to lock my demons away.

I try to hold the memory
The cavern of emotion overflowing
When I first stood at the board,
A teacher, offering safe harbor
Loving those a little rough around the edges
Because I remember my edges being ignored

I tried to notice the ignored.

I try to forget the pain, the terrible loss
Children fighting battles I couldn't win
Students crying in my arms, lost friends
Demons crawling closer as I tried
To maintain normalcy in lessons and tests
Hopes for the future

I tried to maintain hope.

I try to remember every classroom I've left
And forget the reasons why
Every town, every child, every colleague, every friend
Every step that little girl with the nightmares took
In halls that were safe
Until the drills reminded the woman otherwise

I tried to block out the drills.

There are so many things I try
and have tried countless times
To hold myself steady
To maintain the connection
With the one place that felt
Right and safe and like home

I try to write wrongs in words To
imprison them on the page Until
the words won't come

I try to find peace inside walls
Amongst bright faces of potential
Until the walls close in

I try to breath in the laughter of
learning and friendships Until
the laughing sobs

I still keep trying.

MAINTAINING INTEGRITY

Love sacrifices all when
We lack empathy
Compassionate abscondence
Relies on courage
Surrendering nothing so
That integrity
perseveres in dark times...strong

WHO MIGHT WE HAVE BEEN

Who might we have been
If trauma didn't get us first
If nightmares hadn't
Overshadowed dreams
If our bodies had been our own
And our minds had been free
Uncluttered for creativity?

LINGERING EFFECTS

My trauma is old
Tucked away in crates
Beneath sepia portraits
Muffled by colored veils
Under layers of dust
That occasionally
Make me sneeze

My pain is timeless
Fading like scars
Between laugh lines
And debated stretch marks
When the swelling recedes
From my battered psyche
Only to be reborn
In cyclical reminders
That safety is an illusion
Built in the tricks
Our minds play
To protect us from
Nightmares
In human form

My anxiety is forever
Hiding in the crevices
Of happy moments
Waiting
For the next
Press release
To cut loose the tape
Enough for memories
To ooze
From their bindings
Reopening wounds
That wash away The
facade of control I
present to the world

JARRED MEMORIES

memories jarred from
long-forgotten hiding space
glisten with fresh tears

NOT QUITE YET

Sometimes the pain is too much
The memories drown out the day
Worry about what was takes hold
What is has nothing to grip
Caught in the vice, mind reeling
Pills overflowing, dulling the ache;
Hope starts to spring a new day
Better opportunity to forget
Healing thoughts of the future
Marred by scars reopened
All becomes silent, numb
Frozen in time, hopeless
Wishful thinking in liquid courage;
Fighting ghosts of long-dead demons
Promises of earned release
The pain fades again.

SUNSHINE AND SEASHELLS

Lost, tossed, and battered
Seashells wait in shifting sands
For morning's sunrise

KEEPING SILENT

When you were young,
"Shhh...don't tell anyone," and
"It's our little secret," worked to
Manipulate you into conspiracy
Against your own mind and body.
They brought you solace that you were not
Alone.
You were placated into a dream of love
That should have been real based on
Existence alone,
Not your silent tears.

When you were a little older,
Fear and threats of rejection haunted
By those early manipulations and
Unmet need for security tricked you into
Accepting the bare minimum of lust
Disguised as love, of fun
Disguised as friendship,
All serving as reminders that
You are alone,
While you cried silent tears.

As you aged, and the nightmares faded,
The sense of aloneness pushed
You to become more lustful and
Less fulfilled.
Your desire to be "honest" about
your needs manifested in cliche
Professions of enjoying life while
Looking for the one.
The one was an image steeped in
Changing expectations and
Hopes based on broken experiences
Mired in silent tears

Now, with the wisdom of age,
You have found your voice,
The one that speaks for that little girl,
That comforts that tormented adolescent
That fortifies the broken woman with
Boundaries of empathy and compassion
For who they were and what they lived,
Understanding that their tears were not
Silent. Instead, they were screams of injustice
In a world that steals innocence
behind closed doors while screaming about
Public perceptions that belie the truth,
Where being alone is sometimes safer
Than society allows, and finding shelter
Is less about a person or place and more
About your state of being.
Your voice speaks your truth
With an air of accountability,
As you dry your eyes.

PART IV
POEMS OF HOPE

UNSETTLED SPIRIT

The spirit seeks peace
In the arms of a lover
Or the pews of a church

The spirit seeks peace
In chemical oblivion
Or warm salt air

The spirit seeks peace
In a world full of chaos
Or a lifetime of emptiness

I, too, have sought peace
In lovers' arms and
The sacred ritual,
In liquid forgetfulness and
The ocean's breeze,
When my world was chaotic and
When the nothingness overwhelmed

My spirit finds peace
When blank pages meet
Beautiful words in ways
Loving arms,
Hymns of glory,
Shots of redemption,
Waves of emotion,
And the world
Never wrought.

LILACS IN BLOOM

shout out to all the
ate bloomers in lilac hues...
your colors still shine

CLARITY IN THE STORM

I am at my best
when the sky's tumultuous
and my mind is clear

SUSPENDED CHILDHOOD

The patina of weathering
shows the passage of time,
yet we hope to maintain
our innocence,
our delight,
our enthusiasm for life.

Life that consumes our energy,
hones our ambitions,
molds our beliefs, and
hardens our convictions,
until we dream again.

Dreams of a new-found love,
of people,
of art, and
of rest
when our weary souls
hold onto the vestige of a childhood
caught in suspended animation...

if only in our minds.

WRITTEN RECIPE

I ground hurt to meal
mix it with experience
and bake poetry

TATTOO

I want to embed the memory of us
On my skin like a tattoo
Feeling each pinprick of your touch
Like a spark in the dark
Dead of night where we lay
Against each other miles apart
Though neither of us have moved
Lack of intentional intimacy
Gave way to uncomfortable comfort
Our love the warm embrace of an oversized hoodie
Now threadbare and drafty
Worn of its welcome though a welcome memory
Soon bound for the donation box
Easily tossed and forgotten
Unlike a tattoo that may fade but never forgets
The beauty of what once was
Remaining painted as a masterpiece
That says "I had this...once"

DROWSY MINUET

Effervescent dreams
of simpler times
poured into
youthful dance.
Sluggish movements
and stifled yawns
reminders that
time has passed.
The drinks have changed
from mixology to tastings.
The dance has slowed.
The dream, however,
remains vividly lucid.

MISSING PIECES

At life's end, we're buried
Whole yet incomplete
We leave bits of ourselves
Hearts and souls
With those we've loved
Hoping we fit into their puzzles
In the same way we wove
Them into our tapestries
Shrouds of memories
Faded over time
Yet unforgotten.

BRIDGING THE GAP

A memory near faded
A monument of time lost
Leading back on the path
Like a breadcrumb left

A travel-worn road
A traversal of paths
Bridging the gap
Between coming and going

An unfathomable depth
An unsure traveler
Stuck on the outskirts
Searching for the pinnacle

A realization of triumph
A retreat forward moving
Trip of a lifetime
Tempering past hurts

A gratifying relief
A glimpse of shared affection
Present obscures pain
Patching fissures in miles

ON HEALING

Shades of amber clouding my gaze
Tears forming mascara trails
As I replay the conversation,
The inconsideration, the disrespect.

Do I address it?
How do I address it?
When do I address it?
They didn't...they couldn't...
There's no way they could've meant it...
Like that.

Tell them.
What should I say?
Tell them how they made you feel.
What if I imagined it?
Tell them how their words hurt.
What if I hurt them back?
When will you let this be about you?

The words sit on my screen. They
scream out the hurt,
the anger, the insecurities,
the fear of laying it all on the line.

Countless conversations, names
and faces lost to time, whirl
through my mind in a dance of
continuous anxious drumming to
the tune of "Will we make it?" I
press send.

CATERPILLAR DREAMS

caterpillar thoughts
upon nestling in cocoons:
we must all fly free

but first we must melt away
dissolving from existence

WHISPERED WISHES

wishes like whispers
written on a painted sky
dreaming in the midst

HOPEFUL FORGETTING

I wish to forget
the feel of foreboding fate—
now, not if, but when

CREATIVITY'S CANDELABRA

The candelabra of creativity
Words filling frustration's void
Each pillar's healing light
Cutting through the darkness

Authenticity screams for release
In flickers of hope
Melded to the essence of being
Bringing voice to self

Imagination dreams of speculation
Triggering flights of fancy
Where shadows dance in flames
And spark the unexpected

Awareness brings light to the invisible
Arching toward perspectives
Enveloped in obscurity
Yet resplendent reflections of truth

Ashes floating on the wind
Like the release of memories
Too painful to hold
Intertwined in multiple realities

WINNING THE WAR

Trudging through judgment
Invisibly gauging
The impasse most fragile
Educated raging

Injustice abounds
While solace we're chasing
Atrocities unfazed
Make demons worth facing

No longer unnamed
The enemy risen
Humanity's darkness
Our personal prison

In lieu of frailty
Stability unveils
In light of lost knowledge
Salvation prevails

AGING WITH WISDOM

Cracks in the ceiling
Settled with age
Like wrinkles and crow's feet
Setting the stage
For the telling of stories
From the most sage
For wisdom comes slowly
With turns of a page

AM I STILL HERE?

I've come to this space
these lines incomplete
thinking I'd share the turmoil
the confusion taking shape
running rampant
rampantly ruining my calm
composure decomposed
in diagnoses

The perfectly curated mask
like a lightbulb blown
cracked on the inside
visible only when shaken
rattling like skeleton bones
warning that there's more to see
under the surface
iceberg
frozen in fear

Which came first
inattention
hyper-fixation
anxiety
hormonal fluctuations

The when doesn't matter
the how a wasted question
impact making crash dummies of
emotions and productivity
clashing self-perception
with
fun house mirrors
running face first into reality

Words holding court
tennis match
ping-ponging
creativity and silence
brain never silent
screaming in the abyss

Hoping for poetry
in a world built in prose
supported with lies
lying in wait of normalcy
a new normal
a reconciled idea of becoming
redefining what is from what was
in search of what might be from
what was never imagined to find
myself anew

HOPE IS A THING ON WHEELS

Emily Dickinson said,
"Hope is a thing with feathers,"
But really hope is a thing on wheels,
wheels tethered to the ground
with limitless possible destinations
if you've the time and creative mind
to forego the expected stop
and ride a little further
or make a transfer at the local station.

First class, sure bet, sets you up
for a short ride through endless landscape
where second-class people don't exist,
giving a false sense that life's ride is smooth.

Second class, scenic route,
if scenery means quiet streets
through quiet neighborhoods
pristine yards with weathered homes
cared for and broken in, but never broken into
because there's nothing worth taking
except the pride that comes from living
on this side of the tracks.

Third-class honesty, roughly hewn
loud, busy, and authentic
with songs of promise and pain
livestock in the hold and luggage
made from cardboard boxes.
The long way home with the cheapest cost And
the greatest lessons to be learned
where colors are painted on every wall,
portraits of lives lived, hard and true
hopes sprayed across concrete and boxcars
if they sit still too long, if you sit still too long.

Trains, buses, automobiles
endless potential here on Earth
for reaching a destination that makes us feel
comfort, pride, excitement, escape
even if that next transfer, roundabout, or
station brings us right back home again
or gives us a one-way ticket to anywhere else
because tomorrow is another day
another chance to hope.

POETRY IS...

Poetry is healing when the pain is too much.
Poetry is peace when the world is chaotic.
Poetry is love when the emptiness invades.

Poetry is hope that our words will outlive us.
Poetry is trust that the clouds will part.
Poetry is faith that we will persevere.

TRIGGER WARNINGS

I write to heal
because I have been broken
shattered into pieces
forced to glue myself together
mortar mixed with tears
that spill on the page like poetry

I write to forget
the loneliness of abandonment
the times I left myself behind
pursuing acceptance
under guise of friendship
tethering love to feeble minds

I write to forgive
myself the historical aches of
generational slights where
women's worth was tied with rings
compounded in the collateral womb
rather than developmental prowess

I write to remember
moments of joy easily forgotten
placed on a shelf dusty from neglect
moldy albums of smiling photographs
faces of friends left behind
episodes overshadowed by new pains

I write to release
shoulders welded to ears
tension gripped lungs under water
drowning in a sea of regret
searching for the right words
to both lose and find myself in promise

I write to renew
a tattered soul threadbare
from external misuse and internal disuse
left floating in the giveaway pile
too stained to be worthwhile
too valuable for dumping

I write to silence
my own triggers that come without warnings
unwanted as I have felt in love's embrace
intractable as the life I have tried to piece together
unforgiving as the linguistic straight jacket
I wrap them in swaddled like a baby

WRITING MYSELF WHOLE

I never thought I could write
I mean, I know the mechanics—
the grammar and syntax,
punctuation, and diction necessary.
I'd written lauded analyses of others' works,
reading the minds of masters
as if they had spoon fed me their thoughts.
I'd taught students who'd feared their own voices
the power of content over form,
that editing can shape communication
in ways words spoken could scarcely imagine.
I'd presented a thesis on authentic writing
and its value for language development.
I wrote my way through a doctorate,
bringing new life to research with no definitive answers.
Yet, I never thought I could write
because when I sit in front of the blank page,
the words build dams in my flooded mind,
my story a logjam of memories,
both painful and soothing,
unwilling to seep tears through the cracks
of my fingers, as they bang on the keys,
begging the fragments to coalesce
and fill the page, so I can see myself.
I'd never call myself a writer,
And yet, here I am.

ABOUT THE AUTHOR

Bobbie Isabel is a lover of words. She spent her childhood escaping in books and finding solace in the public library. Her career in education circled around language in all its forms (spoken, aural, written, etc.), and she takes all those experiences into account in her writing. As an adult, she finds healing in poetry, exploring themes such as vulnerability and authenticity in her poems. When she's not writing, you can find her in the audience reveling in the language-rich environment of musical theater.

Follow Bobbie all over social media:
https://linktr.ee/bisabelwrites

See her website for the latest updates on all her writing endeavors and a poetry blog:
https://bisabelwrites.com

Coming Soon:
December 2023: Lilli and the Nervous Narwhal
A children's picture adventure book.
Early 2024: The Maenad (Working Title)
A fantasy coming-of-age novel

www.ingramcontent.com/pod-product-compliance
Lightning Source LLC
Chambersburg PA
CBHW031435120626
46545CB00006B/2422